W9-BMJ-532

REMARKABLE
LGBTQ
LIVES™

Ellen
DeGENERES

TELEVISION'S FUNNIEST HOST

REMARKABLE LGBTQ LIVES™

Ellen DeGENERES

TELEVISION'S FUNNIEST HOST

BARBARA GOTTFRIED HOLLANDER

ROSEN PUBLISHING®

New York

Published in 2015 by The Rosen Publishing Group, Inc.
29 East 21st Street, New York, NY 10010

Copyright © 2015 by The Rosen Publishing Group, Inc.

First Edition

All rights reserved. No part of this book may be reproduced in any form without permission in writing from the publisher, except by a reviewer.

Library of Congress Cataloging-in-Publication Data

Hollander, Barbara Gottfried.
Ellen DeGeneres: television's funniest host/Barbara Gottfried Hollander.—First edition.
    pages cm.—(Remarkable LGBTQ lives)
Includes bibliographical references and index.
ISBN 978-1-4777-7895-1 (library bound)
1. DeGeneres, Ellen—Juvenile literature.
2. Comedians—United States—Biography—
Juvenile literature. 3. Television personalities—
United States—Biography—Juvenile literature.
I. Title.
PN2287.D358H65 2015
792.702'8092—dc23
[B]
                                        2014010943

Manufactured in China

CONTENTS

INTRO

I n [my] dream, I was holding a tiny finch in the palm of my hand. I could feel how much I loved this bird and that it was safe in my hand, and I was reaching in to put it back in its cage—one of these thin, bamboo, beautiful, multitiered cages—and as I was putting the bird back in, I realized that the cage was against a window and the bird could fly out. The bird realized it at the same time I did, and I became the bird. And the bird looked at me and wanted to fly out, but I looked at the bird and said, "But you're safe in here in a beautiful cage. Don't leave." And the bird just looked at me and flew out the window.

Ellen DeGeneres shared her dream with Oprah Winfrey in an exclusive *O, The Oprah Magazine* interview. Today, Ellen DeGeneres is one of the most famous people in America: television icon, host and executive producer of *The Ellen DeGeneres Show* (among the most highly rated shows worldwide), recipient of dozens of awards—from the Mark Twain Prize for American Humor to the Human Rights Campaign's first National Civil Rights Award—and one of *Forbes'* 100 Most Powerful Women and *Time* magazine's 100 most influential people. The list goes on. But her life was not always like the slogan she utters as a CoverGirl spokesperson, "Easy, breezy, beautiful."

In 1982, Ellen DeGeneres was named Showtime's Funniest Person in America. More than thirty years later, she is still making America laugh.

At one time, DeGeneres harbored a secret that she feared would destroy her career. Her mother, Betty DeGeneres, also worried about people's negative reactions to her daughter's secret. Both women knew of the intolerance and discrimination that confronted gay people in both their private and professional lives. In the 1980s and '90s, DeGeneres was climbing the ladder of professional success. She was the first female stand-up comic to sit down on *The Tonight Show Starring Johnny Carson.* She was named Showtime's Funniest Person in America and starred in her own show. People liked her.

Would she risk it all by sharing her secret with America? Did she truly feel safe in a "thin, bamboo, beautiful, multitiered cage"? In 1997, DeGeneres took the courageous step of publicly announcing that she was gay. Like the bird in her dream, DeGeneres chose to fly out the window and soared higher than she ever thought possible. In that same *O* interview, DeGeneres shared, "You know, people say, 'Why do you have to tell everybody [that you are gay], who cares, and why do you have to announce it?' It's because it's your truth and the truth shall set you free."

CHAPTER 1

THE EARLY YEARS

"People always ask me, 'Were you funny as a child?' Well, no, I was an accountant."—*Ellen DeGeneres*, Goodreads

Ellen DeGeneres was a baby, a child, and of course a teenager before she was one of the nation's funniest people. In her early years, DeGeneres was close to her mom, spent time with her dad, and admired her brother. She had good times and bad times. At a young age, DeGeneres learned about the power of laughter: how it made the good times even better and the bad times more bearable.

IN THE BEGINNING...

Ellen Lee DeGeneres's life began in a suburb of New Orleans, Louisiana, called Metaire. She was born barefoot, not in her trademark blue sneakers, on January 26, 1958. As a child, Ellen traveled by bike. "I rode my bike everywhere," DeGeneres told Liz

Scott of *New Orleans Magazine.* "All over the campus [of Newcomb College]. All over uptown. You know, people can grow up in New Orleans without realizing how unique a city it is. I remember thinking that it was a really neat place." Ellen's mother and grand- mother were also born in this nifty place.

Ellen's mother, Betty, was a speech patholo- gist, and her father, Elliot, sold insurance. In Lisa Iannucci's book *Ellen DeGeneres: A Biography,* Betty shares that Elliot believed one child was enough. But Betty begged for another, whom she first called "a beautiful blob of fatness" and later a "miracle" named Ellen or "El." Ellen liked to watch television shows, such as *I Love Lucy, The Dick Van Dyke Show,* and *The Ed Sullivan Show.* She liked comedians, including Bob and Ray, George Gobel, and Jack Benny. Ellen also loved animals and imagined studying them in Africa, just like famous zoologist Dian Fossey.

Ellen's parents were both religious members of the Church of Christ, Scientist, a church created by Mary Baker Eddy about two hundred years ago. Ellen's mom eventually left the church. In 1971, she also left Elliot and rented a two-bedroom apart- ment in Lake Vista, a New Orleans neighborhood. Ellen's older brother, Vance, had his own room, and Ellen and her mom shared a bedroom with Ellen's pet snake. Ellen turned to comic relief to ease her mother's pain from the marital separation. In a 2006

Wearing her trademark blue Converse sneakers, Ellen DeGeneres accepts a People's Choice Award. By 2014, she had won fourteen of these awards.

As a teenager, Ellen realized the healing nature of humor as she helped her mother cope with divorce.

issue of *Teen People*, DeGeneres explained, "I was helping [my mother] cope with a broken heart. It brought us closer together and made me realize the power of humor."

In *St. James Encyclopedia of Popular Culture*, DeGeneres also shared, "My mother was going through some really hard times and I could see when she was really getting down, and I would start to make fun of her dancing. Then she'd start to laugh and I'd make fun of her laughing. And she'd laugh so hard she'd start to cry, and then I'd make fun of that. So I would totally bring her from where I'd seen her start going into depression to all the way out of it." In her book *Love, Ellen: A Mother/Daughter Journey*, Betty DeGeneres adds, "Our difficulties [arising from the divorce] strengthened our [mother-daughter] bond."

Ellen and her mom became very close in the years following the divorce, especially when Vance's music career kept him on the road. So Ellen and her mom were a "twosome, enjoying each other's company," according to *Love, Ellen*. These special times would include shopping and eating cheesecake at Camellia Grill. Betty confirmed that Ellen's humor was a coping mechanism for both of them. In her book, Betty recounts other displays of Ellen's affection, such as asking her mom's coworkers to be extra nice on her mom's birthday.

THE MEN IN ELLEN'S LIFE

Vance is not only Ellen's older brother, he is also an entertainer who got a break as a bass player in a band called the Cold. This New Orleans–based band was very popular in the southeastern United States. The Cold released two albums and several singles between 1980 and 1985. Her brother's success provided additional incentive for Ellen to pursue her comedy-related ambitions. "Everybody knew who he [Vance] was," she told *People* magazine. "That's what motivated me to do something, because I watched him get all this attention and glory."

Ellen shared some childhood thoughts with Bridget Foley in *W Magazine*, including that she was "afraid of anything" and that she always wanted to feel special, liked, and famous. "I thought if I could find a way to be famous [like my brother]," she said, "people would love me."

Another thing that Ellen wanted to have was enough money. In her book *The Funny Thing Is...* she wrote that her father would spend Saturdays and Sundays looking at real estate that they could not afford, such as two-bedroom homes in more expensive neighborhoods. One time, Ellen and her dad went to a car showroom. Ellen sat in the cars and imagined that her family owned them. But her father had no intention of buying a car. When he finally told her they were just looking, Ellen could no longer follow the "unspoken ban on expressing emotion in our family." And she cried. Her father looked away and gave her something to dry her tears. But it was too late. Ellen knew what it felt like to express her feelings, and there was no turning back.

TRAGEDIES

Ellen's parents separated in 1971, and the divorce was finalized at last in 1973. The following year, Ellen's mom remarried another salesman, who is only referred to as "B" by both Ellen and her mother. Ellen was about sixteen years old at the time of her mother's remarriage. Ellen, her mom, and her new stepdad moved to Atlanta, Texas, about four hundred miles from New Orleans. Vance decided to stay with their biological father, while Ellen lived in a town that she describes in Lisa Iannucci's book as having a "confining atmosphere." Still, Ellen was liked in high school and joined the tennis team.

The year of the move, Ellen's mom was diag-nosed with breast cancer. She went into Wadley

Hospital for surgical treatment, receiving a radical modified mastectomy, which is the removal of a breast and most of the lymph nodes under the arm. While her mother was in the hospital, Ellen's stepfather sexually molested her. This means that he used force or threats to engage Ellen in unwanted sexual acts. In the first incident, B told Ellen that her mom might have another breast cancer lump and he needed to feel Ellen's breasts for comparison.

Shortly after the first incident, B tried to molest her again, in spite of Ellen's verbal protests. Another time, Ellen only escaped when she "kicked a window out...[and slept] in a hospital" after he "tried to break down the door to my bedroom," she told *Allure* magazine. DeGeneres kept the molestation a secret for more than thirty years. In 2005, DeGeneres broke her silence. She urges teenage girls to say no to unwanted sexual acts and to speak up if molestation occurs.

BACK HOME

When Ellen moved, she transferred from Grace King High School in Louisiana to Atlanta High School in Texas. To celebrate her thirty-year class reunion in 2006, Ellen flew her graduating class out to California to appear as guests on her hugely popular television program, *The Ellen DeGeneres*

THE DEGENERES FAMILY MOVES TO LOS ANGELES

When Ellen lived in San Francisco, she hoped to move to Los Angeles eventually to pursue a television and movie career. In September 1985, Ellen moved to L.A. and was soon joined by her brother, Vance. He hoped to pursue his music career in California and teamed up with Gina Schock of the popular girl band the Go-Go's. After the L.A. move, Ellen continued to do stand-up comedy, landing a gig at Caesar's Palace in Las Vegas, Nevada.

Ellen's mom visited her and Vance in Los Angeles. In 1990, at the age of sixty, Betty joined her children. She found a job with an L.A. speech pathologist company. Ellen and her partner, Jan, found a place for Betty to live. When Betty arrived in L.A. after a long road trip, she was greeted by Ellen, Jan, Vance, and his wife, Mimi. In her book, Betty wrote, "If home is where the heart is, I was home."

Show. She also presented her former high school with an electronic LED marquee sign.

Ellen then attended the University of New Orleans as a communication major, but she left after just one semester. In her 2009 Tulane University commencement address, she wisecracked, "I didn't go to any college at all. Any college. And I'm not saying you wasted your time, or money, but look at me, I'm a huge celebrity." She also mentioned learning courage from the "school of hard knocks," and added "some of the most devastating things that happen to you will teach you the most."

Ellen DeGeneres delivers the commencement speech to Tulane University's graduating class of 2009.

After leaving college, Ellen's first job was working in a law firm with her cousin. Then, she had other jobs in her late teens and early twenties. In her book *Love, Ellen*, Betty recalls Ellen's job as a placement counselor at an employment agency called Snellings & Snellings in New Orleans. Twenty-year-old Ellen happily told her mom that she had attained the number one spot in fees generated. But Ellen was still worried about paying the bills, and she longed to buy a car to ease the two-mile walk to work. After a few months at the employment agency, Ellen left and started a new job as a sales clerk at the Dixie Art Supplies store.

Other New Orleans–based jobs included painting houses, selling clothes and vacuum cleaners, and working in restaurants as a waitress, hostess, oyster shucker, and bartender. Years later, in 2012, Ellen returned to one of her first jobs at J.C. Penney in Metaire and aired the visit on her television show. Then, she presented everyone in the audience with a $100 J.C. Penney gift card.

VANCE DEGENERES: ELLEN'S BROTHER

Vance DeGeneres was born in New Orleans on September 2, 1954. New Orleans was home until New York and California offered more opportunities in the world of music. Vance was a bass player for the band the Cold. Later, he was also a guitarist for a band called House of Schock, which included Gina Schock, drummer for the pop band the

(Left to right) Executive producer Vance DeGeneres, actor Steve Buscemi, and executive producer Charlie Hartock attend New Line Cinema's world premiere of *The Incredible Burt Wonderstone.*

Go-Go's. In 1988, Schock and Vance DeGeneres formed House of Schock and wrote an entire album with songs such as "Middle of Nowhere," "Where Love Goes," and "Just to Dream." Vance was also

a composer for the 1991 short film comedy *The Walter Ego* and a participant in the sound tracks for the 1988 films *The Accused* and *Bull Durham.*

Vance's scriptwriting credits include TV episodes of *Ellen* ("Clip Show Patient" and "Bowl, Baby, Bowl"), *Gary the Rat*, *The Secret World of Alex Mack*, *Diagnosis Murder*, and *Eerie, Indiana.* Vance also wrote material for several award shows, such as *The 79th Annual Academy Awards* (2007), *The Annual Grammy Awards* (1997), and *The 46th Annual Primetime Emmy Awards* (1994). In 2007, Ellen DeGeneres hosted *The 79th Annual Academy Awards*, the very show her brother helped write. She also hosted the Oscars in 2014.

Today, Vance is best known for his movie and television work. He was an actor on episodes of several shows, such as *Ellen* (1995–1997), *The Ellen Show* (2002), and *Gary the Rat* (2003). He also appeared in videos such as *Mr. Bill Goes to Washington* (1993) and *Oh Noooooo! It's Mr. Bill's 20th Anniversary* (1995); the main character, Mr. Bill, is a Play-Doh character created by Walter Williams and got started when Williams won a 1976 home movie contest sponsored by the late-night comedy show *Saturday Night Live*. Vance also appeared in *The Not Goods Anthology: This Is Absolutely Not Good* (2010), and in 2013, Vance played a reporter in Cambodia in the movie *The Incredible Burt Wonderstone*.

Vance's experience in television and film also includes producing. He was the executive producer of *The Incredible Burt Wonderstone* and several television shows, including twenty episodes of *Inside Comedy* from 2012 to 2013 and the 2001 television series *Rendez-View*. Vance was also the supervising producer of the 2011 film *Crazy, Stupid, Love*, the television series *Pat Croce: Moving* In (2004), *Late World with Zach*, and a 2003 episode of *The 5th Wheel*.

From 1999 to 2001, Vance was a correspondent on Comedy Central's *The Daily Show with Jon Stewart*.

This Emmy and Peabody Award–winning program looks at politics, technology, trends, pop culture, and sports and entertainment through comedic eyes. As part of the show, Vance appeared with well-known actor and writer Steve Carell on Indecision 2000 campaign coverage, providing comedic analysis of the debate between then Texas governor George W. Bush and Vice President Al Gore. According to an article by Kurt Jensen, Vance described his roles of writing and acting as "just about perfect." In 2014, Vance was copresident of comedian Steve Carell's production company at Warner Bros., called Carousel Productions.

CHAPTER 2

AIM BIG

"Never follow anyone else's path, unless you're in the woods and you're lost and you see a path. Then by all means follow that path."—Ellen DeGeneres, Goodreads

Sometimes, the hardest moments in our lives create the biggest opportunities. One of Ellen DeGeneres's most difficult times prompted her to make a life-changing goal, which eventually launched her into the world of comedy. DeGeneres continued to climb the professional ladder from stand-up comedy to the world of television. But DeGeneres was keeping a big secret from her audience—a secret that she had shared with her mother at the age of twenty.

DIVINE CONVERSATION

Ellen's response to another tragic event propelled her toward becoming a top female comedian. In

1980, she was living in a basement apartment. As DeGeneres recalled in her 2009 Tulane commencement speech, "I had no money, I had no heat, no air, I had a mattress on the floor and the apartment was infested with fleas." As if that weren't enough, during this time, her girlfriend, poet Kathy Perkoff, was killed in a car accident. DeGeneres passed by the accident but didn't stop. "I didn't know it was her and I kept going, and I found out shortly after that, it was her."

In her book *Eat, Pray, Love,* author Elizabeth Gilbert recalls being on the floor when she was in an emotionally challenging place. Gilbert turned to God, and this moment became a pivotal point in her life. DeGeneres also reacted to a get-off-the-floor moment by having an imaginary phone conversation with God. As she later described, her comical conversation prompted a major life goal: "I'm gonna do this [the conversation] on *The Tonight Show With Carson*...and I'm gonna be the first woman [comic] in the history of the show to be called over to sit down."

On November 18, 1986, DeGeneres performed her conversation with God in front of an audience. In the skit, DeGeneres asks God why fleas exist. It was the same question that she posed years earlier, when her girlfriend died, while the fleas in her mattress lived. DeGeneres provided a comical answer involving the flea collar and spray industries. Her

Ellen DeGeneres paved the way for females to sit down on *The Tonight Show Starring Johnny Carson*. Here, Johnny Carson talks to comedian Joan Rivers.

act was a hit! That night, DeGeneres became the first woman in the show's history to sit down on *The Tonight Show Starring Johnny Carson.* As DeGeneres says on a *Huffpost* video, being on *The Tonight Show* "was all part of the plan."

STAND-UP COMEDY

Before DeGeneres got a Johnny Carson couch invite, she did stand-up comedy in small clubs, big clubs, and coffee-houses, which means that she performed comedy alone on stage in front of a live audience. In 1981, DeGeneres was emcee at Clyde's Comedy Club in New Orleans, where she performed her first monologue, "A Phone Call to God." Later, DeGeneres took her comedy act on the road. While traveling around the country, she

Ellen DeGeneres appeared more than thirty times on *The Tonight Show with Jay Leno.*

performed at Crackers Comedy Club in Indianapolis, which has also hosted comedians such as Jay Leno, Dennis Miller, and Chris Rock.

In her book *My Point... And I Do Have One*, DeGeneres humorously recalls a Showtime contest she entered in 1982 for Funniest Person in New Orleans with her "A Phone Call to God" skit. She was one of about sixteen people in the competition. That night, DeGeneres was sick with fever, but she went on stage anyway. She won, and her performance was taped, and she won Funniest Person in America. The win opened many doors and prompted a move to San Francisco, California. As DeGeneres comments, "[The contest] wasn't like Miss America. There were no tough questions like 'How would you use your title as The Funniest Person in America to help world peace? And the talent portion of the show was...being funny."

After moving to San Fransisco, DeGeneres still performed in comedy clubs in different parts of the country. When she worked comedy clubs in Dallas, her mom joined her for support.

By 1986, with the help of Jay Leno, DeGeneres was offered that history-making spot on Johnny Carson's show. On *The Tonight Show with Jay Leno*, DeGeneres told Leno and his audience, "Leno is responsible for me being booked on 'The Tonight Show' with Johnny Carson, because you told the booker, Jim McCawley, to stay at The Improv [in Las Vegas, Nevada] and watch me. You said, 'This girl's great'...so thank you very much for everything you've done. You're amazing. You're a good guy...You always tried to help me in every way."

Throughout her career, DeGeneres has been making audiences shake with laughter as a regular guest on shows such as *The Tonight Show with Jay Leno, The Late Show with David Letterman, The Oprah Winfrey Show, Later with Greg Kinnear, Larry King Live*, and *Good Morning America*. In 1991, DeGeneres received the Female Comedy Club Stand-Up Comic of the Year award.

SHARING HER FEAR

With her mom's support, DeGeneres took the comedy world by storm, earning awards and top performance spots. In her Tulane commencement speech,

At the age of twenty, DeGeneres told her mom that she was gay. In time, her mom became one of the biggest advocates of LGBT rights.

DeGeneres said, "And I started this path of stand-up and it was successful and it was great, but it was hard, because I was trying to please everybody and I had this secret that I was keeping, that I was gay. And I thought if people found out, they wouldn't like me, they wouldn't laugh at me."

In 1976, at the age of eighteen, DeGeneres realized that she was gay, or sexually attracted to people of the same gender. Later, in her blogs, DeGeneres wrote that she dated several boys in high school, but she never

PREJUDICE FACED BY GAY PEOPLE IN THE 1970S TO '80S

In the late 1970s, DeGeneres shared her sexual orientation with her mom. Both Degeneres and her mom feared the reactions of others because during the 1970s and 1980s, societal attitudes toward gay people included intolerance, prejudice, insensitivity, and ignorance. People failed to see sexual orientation as a legitimate lifestyle option.

In a paper, *Stigma, Prejudice, and Violence Against Lesbians and Gay Men*, Gregory M. Herek reported the following:

- Two-thirds of people living in the United States in the 1970s and 1980s condemned homosexuality.
- Twenty-five percent of people would strongly object to working with a gay person (1987 Roper Poll).
- Twenty-seven percent of people would rather not work with a gay person (1987 Roper Poll).
- Only 47% percent of people believed homosexual acts between consenting adults should be legal (1989 Gallup Poll [Colasanto]).

Gay men and women faced discrimination in both their personal and private lives:

- In the 1970s, Anita Bryant and her "Save the Children" organization successfully launched a campaign in Dade County, Florida, to repeal an ordinance that prevented antigay discrimination.
- According to *Marriage Rights and Gay Rights: Interpreting the Constitution* by Barbara Gottfried Hollander, "The 1986 court case *Bowers v. Hardwick*, upheld laws that told gay couples how to behave sexually in the privacy of their own homes."
- Before 1975, the American Psychological Association (APA) defined homosexuality as a mental illness.

It would take another few decades for America to develop sensitivity and acceptance for gay couples and gay marriage. The struggle for equal treatment for all sexual orientations continues, with Ellen and Betty DeGeneres as staunch advocates.

felt fulfilled with the relationships. DeGeneres eventually realized that she was gay and later refers to Kathy Perkoff, whom she met when she was twenty-one and Perkoff was twenty-three, as the "first love of her life." The sadness felt after Perkoff tragic death inspired Ellen's "A Phone Call to God" skit, which she ultimately viewed as a "gift from Kathy."

At summer's end in 1978, on a walk near the West Beach Boulevard in Pass Christian, Mississippi, DeGeneres shared her secret with her mom. At the age of twenty, she uttered the words, "Mom, I'm gay." In her book *Love, Ellen*, Betty writes that it was "the biggest shock of my life and the last thing I expected to hear." Betty feared for her daughter's welfare, given the negativity and prejudice confronting gay people. DeGeneres's declaration was followed by an open discussion of her feelings and experiences.

Betty would eventually tell her daughter, "You are my child and I will love you unconditionally no matter what." In her book, Betty shares that she went through a process to understand that sexual orientation is not a choice and that "being gay is normal and healthy." She also realized that she had to let go of her own expectations and "in their place, room was being made for the truth, about her [Ellen] and about me."

In time, the truth would hold many lessons about being gay, brave, and loving. And in more time, Betty would realize that Ellen's coming out (telling others about her sexual orientation) was a gift. Coming out presents the opportunity for a gay child and his or her parent to express their true selves. As motivational speaker Jack Canfield once wrote, "Everything you want is on the other side of fear."

NEXT UP: TELEVISION

After her first, groundbreaking appearance on *The Tonight Show Starring Johnny Carson*, DeGeneres appeared four more times on the show in the next six months. But it was in 1989 that DeGeneres landed a regular television role on the Fox sitcom *Duet* and its spin-off *Open House*. She played Margo Van Meter, a sarcastic, spunky secretary at an L.A. real estate firm. Despite reviews such as "the laughs come fast and furious" by *New York Daily News* critic Kay Gardella, the show was cancelled the following year.

In 1990 and 1992, DeGeneres appeared in two different HBO comedy specials and was nominated for a Cable ACE Award for her HBO *Command Performance: One Night Stand.* In 1991, she was also in a documentary called *Wisecracks*, which featured female comedians. The women-only show sparked discussion about the role of gender in stand-up comedy. In *Ellen: The Real Story of Ellen DeGeneres*, Kathleen Tracy quotes DeGeneres as saying, "I think I'm a feminist in the sense that I believe women should be equal to men, and it's a ridiculous notion that somebody would think that we're not. But to me that's not being a feminist; it's being a humanist."

In 1992, DeGeneres landed a role as a nurse named Nancy MacIntyre on the ABC show *Laurie Hill*, but the show was canceled shortly after it aired. Still, she and her mom remained "incurable optimists." Little did they know that a big break was right around the corner. ABC Television offered DeGeneres her own series called *These Friends of Mine*, which was scheduled to begin taping in fall 1993. Creators of this half-hour sitcom included David S. Rosenthal— who would go on to be executive producer of *Gilmore Girls* and *The Middle*—and *The Wonder Years* writers, Neal Marlens and Carol Black.

IT'S A HIT!

The show aired in 1994 and was renamed *Ellen* in its second season. DeGeneres played a bookstore owner who tries to get through life with friends and family including the following:

- Friendly Paige, played by Joely Fisher
- Photographer Adam, played by Arye Gross
- Cousin Spence, played by Jeremy Piven

Ellen DeGeneres wins at the 49th Annual Primetime Emmy Awards.

- Coffee guy Joe, played by David Anthony Higgins
- Analytical Audrey, played by Clea Lewis
- Parents Lois and Harold, played by Alice Hirson and Steven Gilborn, respectively

The pilot featured Ellen trying to change her driver's license photograph, while Holly meets a guy named Roger in the motor vehicle line.

According to IMDb, *Ellen* received twenty-eight award nominations and ten wins from the following award organizations:

- Golden Globes, USA
- Primetime Emmy Awards
- Screen Actors Guild Awards
- American Comedy Awards, USA
- BMI Film & TV Awards
- Casting Society of America, USA
- Directors Guild of America, USA
- GLAAD Media Awards
- Peabody Awards
- Satellite Awards
- TV Land Awards
- Viewers for Quality Television Awards
- Writers Guild of America, USA
- Young Artist Awards

Ellen was a hit!

Ellen first hosted the Emmy Awards with *Home Improvement* actress Patricia Richardson.

Her show's success was accompanied by more work and award recognition. In 1994, DeGeneres cohosted the Emmy Awards with Patricia Richardson from *Home Improvement.* Both DeGeneres's mom and dad were there to cheer her on. In her book, *Love, Ellen*, Betty raves, "She was incredible." The *Los Angeles Daily News* reported, "Indeed, a star [Ellen] was born..." From 1995 to '97, Ellen DeGeneres was nominated for Emmy honors such as Outstanding Guest Actress for a Comedy Series in *The Larry Sanders Show* and Outstanding Individual Performance in a Variety or Music Program for *The 38th Annual Grammy Awards.*

CHAPTER 3

THE HUMOROUS HUMANIST

"I learned compassion from being discriminated against. Everything bad that's ever happened to me has taught me compassion."—Ellen DeGeneres, The Oprah Winfrey Show

I n an interview with Oprah Winfrey, Ellen DeGeneres compared herself to a caged bird. When it was time to leave the cage, DeGeneres found her courage. At first, much of the country did not respond well to DeGeneres's flight. Rather than find acceptance, DeGeneres ended up facing her worst fears. She was treated with tremendous disrespect—all because of her sexual orientation.

SHARING WITH MOM

When she moved to Los Angeles, Betty's generous nature was seen in her volunteer work at Project Angel Food, Jewish Family Services, and the Jeffrey Goodman AIDS Clinic. But her greatest joy was

Ellen and Betty DeGeneres
support many causes.
The Gentle Barn brings
together rescued animals
and mainstream and
special needs children in
a healing and safe place.

being "Ellen's unapologetic number one fan," she shares in her *Love, Ellen* book. Betty attended almost every taping of the *Ellen* show. Betty writes, "Even before filming, she [Ellen] would often have me read the script to tell her what I thought. She knows she can always count on me to be honest; just as I can count on her."

Ellen shared the spotlight with her mom. Betty appeared on promos for *Comedy Central* and *These Friends of Mine.* She was also in *Ellen* and her daughter's first movie, *Mr. Wrong.* Betty was very proud of both of her children. In *Love, Ellen*, Betty recounts a trip to Italy (a gift from Ellen). The people on the trip asked Betty if she had any children. She answered, "Yes, I have two... A son, Vance, who writes for television and movies...Right now, he's working on *Ellen*, the T.V. show." People in the group were big fans of the show. One person said, "You're lucky to have such a successful son. And what about you other kid?" to which Betty replied, "Oh, she's Ellen."

Both Ellen and Betty were happy with Ellen's success. But, Ellen wanted to be able to publicly express her sexuality, as heterosexuals already freely did. She wanted to come out and embrace being gay. In *Love, Ellen*, Betty recalls asking Ellen, "Why rock the boat?" Ellen replied, "This is something I have to do." In a *W Magazine* interview with Bridget Foley, Ellen later shared, "I'm openly gay and that I'm not ashamed of it, I'm proud of it... I think secrets are what make you sick." Betty's next step was clear: "to support her all the way. I saw that her own struggles, her fears, and her weariness at having to hide part of herself had influenced her choice. And I saw that she was resolved and determined, prepared to accept the consequences."

Betty reminded herself of the some of the Universal Declaration of Human Rights articles:

- All people are "born free and equal in dignity and rights" (Article 1).
- All people have "the right to freedom of opinion and expression" (Article 19).

The question was: Did others believe that all people were entitled to these human rights? Were Americans, including her biggest fans, willing to accept DeGeneres's sexuality in the same way they accepted heterosexual relationships? Or would she face discrimination just because she was gay?

COMING OUT

The *Ellen* show did more than launch DeGeneres's television career; it served as a platform for her to go public with being gay. On the *Ellen* show, she plays a character named Ellen Morgan, who spent many episodes making life decisions about men. Later, while many of Ellen Morgan's friends get married and have children, Morgan focuses on new business ideas for her bookstore. DeGeneres decided that her character was ready to announce that she was gay.

Ellen's TV character shares her sexual orientation during an episode with Oprah Winfrey.

In August 1996, DeGeneres pitched the idea to the writers and producers of Disney. She needed ABC and Disney on board, but the original response was "maybe." The next month, the *Hollywood Reporter*

grabbed hold of the news, which turned into headlines across the world, such as *Curve Magazine's* "Will the Real Ellen Please Stand Up!" and *Entertainment Weekly's* "Gay TV—Will Ellen DeGeneres' Alter Ego Come Out with Her Hands Up?" By March 1997, the script for "The Puppy Episode" (coming out episode) got the green light.

On April 30, 1997, *Ellen* aired "The Puppy Episode." It drew 42 million viewers and eventually won a Peabody Award. In this episode, Ellen has a dialogue with her therapist, played by Oprah Winfrey:

Ellen: It's not like I'm looking for perfection, I just want to find somebody special, somebody that I click with.

Therapist: Has there ever been anyone you felt you clicked with? What was his name?

Ellen: Susan.

Laughter and applause followed.

TV Land would give " The Puppy Episode" ten out of ten in historical significance and twenty-first place out of Top 100 Sitcom Episodes of All Time. *TV Guide* placed it number thirty-five of the 100 Greatest TV Episodes of All Time. It featured stars such as Oprah Winfrey, Demi Moore, Laura Dern, Billy Bob Thornton, and Melissa Etheridge. But "The Puppy Episode" also had tremendous backlash for DeGeneres and many guest actors and actresses. Oprah Winfrey received hateful letters and phone calls. Meanwhile, Laura Dern could not get work for one and a half years after the episode ran. *Ellen* lasted one more season, with each episode carrying a "parental advisory" warning.

Two weeks before the episode aired, DeGeneres had appeared on the cover of *Time* magazine on April 14 with the words, "Yep, I'm gay." She also announced her sexual orientation on *The Oprah Winfrey Show.* Then, DeGeneres was faced with the public's negative reactions, which included banning DeGeneres from most work for three years. In 2001, DeGeneres and CBS tried to bring back the show, renamed *The Ellen Show*, without making the main character's sexual orientation the main focus. But the show was cancelled after only one season, due to low ratings and few advertisers.

ELLEN'S GIRLFRIENDS

From 1997 to 2000, Ellen dated actress Anne Heche. Heche was in the soap opera *Another World* and movies including *An Ambush of Ghosts*, *Donnie Brasco*, *Volcano*, *Wag the Dog*, and *Six Days, Seven Nights*. She was also on Broadway and had her own series called *Men in Trees*. Heche told Oprah Winfrey, "When I saw Ellen across the room [at a *Vanity Fair* post-Oscars party], I just, like, swung across on the chandelier, and dropped down beside her. Our souls connected. I don't feel like I'm gay. I just feel like I'm in love."

Although Heche once announced her intention to marry Ellen if Vermont legalized gay marriage, the couple eventually broke up after three and a half years together. The following year, Ellen began dating photographer Alexandra Hedison. Hedison acted and directed in films such as *Max Is Missing*, *The Rich Man's Wife*, and *In the Dog House*. Her television performances include ABC's *Prey*, Fox's *L.A. Firefighters*, and A&E's *Designing Blind*. Ellen and Hedison's relationship lasted almost four years. They announced their breakup in Advocate.com, stressing continued mutual support of one another.

THE SAD REALITY

On December 1, 1998, in an interview with *The Southeast Missourian*, DeGeneres shared, "Everything that I ever feared happened to me. I lost my show.... I went from making a lot of money on a sitcom to making no money...knowing that I had been treated so disrespectfully for no other reason than I was gay, I just went into this deep, deep depression." Ellen

Oprah Winfrey was one of several actors who faced a negative backlash from participating in "The Puppy Episode."

DeGeneres was the same person before and after coming out, but much of America now viewed her differently, just because she publicly embraced her sexual orientation. Heterosexuals were able to freely express their sexual orientation without negative consequences, but acceptance for being gay was not the prevailing attitude in much of the country.

It was a time when the Don't Ask, Don't Tell (DADT) policy applied in the U.S. military. This policy stated that gay men and women could serve in the military as long as they hid their sexual orientation. Qualified men and women who were open about being gay could be dismissed from the military. Furthermore, the policy stated that people who "demonstrated a propensity or intent to engage in homosexual acts would create an unacceptable risk to the high standards of morale, good order and discipline, and unit cohesion, which are the essence of military capability."

Just a few years before DeGeneres came out, 54 percent of Colorado's voters passed Amendment 2, which supported state-sanctioned discrimination based on sexual orientation. In response, eight-hundred thousand to one million people had rallied in the March on Washington for Lesbian, Gay, and Bisexual Equal Rights and Liberation. This was also a protest against rising hate crimes directed at lesbian, gay, bisexual, and transgender (LGBT) people. It

HOW DOES INTOLERANCE AND DISCRIMINATION AFFECT LGBT STUDENTS?

Gay teens have been negatively affected by the discrimination they face because of their sexual orientation. The website Healthline cited a 2009 survey of more than seven thousand LGBT students between of the ages thirteen and twenty-one, which found the following:

- Eight out of ten lesbian, gay, bisexual, transgender (LGBT) students were verbally harassed.
- Four in ten LGBT students were physically harassed.
- One in five LGBT students was physically assaulted.
- Six in ten LGBT students felt unsafe in school.

In addition, LGBT students who have faced discrimination are more likely to be depressed, use drugs, and attempt suicide. The American Library Association provides resources for LGBT teens (http://www.ala.org/glbtrt/popularresources/bullying). These resources can help teens who face bullying, suicidal thoughts, and other challenges arising from victimization. The site also provides guidance and support for building a gender sensitive and inclusive environment.

The It Gets Better project provides hope and guidance for LGBT youth. Its efforts strive to create a world that is more supportive of people of all sexual orientations. In his It Gets Better Project video, President Obama told LGBT students, "You are not alone. You didn't do anything wrong. You didn't do anything to deserve being bullied. And there is a whole world waiting for you, filled with possibilities...The other thing you need to know is, things will get better."

would take another seven years after DeGeneres came out before gay marriage would even become legal in the first U.S. state: Massachusetts.

DeGeneres was ahead of her time, and she faced the music. In a *W Magazine* interview with Bridget Foley, DeGeneres admitted, "Magazines were tearing me apart; I was the punch line. I guess that's why I'm so sensitive about negative comedy, because I was the butt of every joke. I was the punch line, and it hurt." In hindsight, DeGeneres continued, "I expected everybody to understand right away. I still think I was right. But I got to learn how to sit back and watch other people and learn what judgment was and have compassion. And learn that not only was I strong enough to make it in the first place, but I was strong enough to come back and make it again."

LGBT COMMUNITY REACTS

An interview with broadcast journalist Diane Sawyer following DeGeneres's coming out helped to facilitate a comeback by opening the door for love, acceptance, and tolerance of the LGBT community. The *Primetime* interview with Diane Sawyer was planned to air right after "The Puppy Episode." Sawyer wanted to interview the whole family and even went to DeGeneres's house for an earlier photo shoot. Betty told Diane Sawyer about the mother-daughter conversation when DeGeneres came out almost twenty years prior.

Ellen DeGeneres and broadcast journalist Diane Sawyer attend the 2006 Annual Matrix Awards, which honors extraordinary women.

Following the interview, Betty became a spokesperson for "love, support, and acceptance" for the LGBT community. As she recalls in her *Love, Ellen* book, her first fan mail read, "This is a note just for you, from a group of girls that watched the *Primetime* interview and wanted to say we would ALL be proud to call you Mom." Many gay men and women approached Betty in public places and wanted to share their stories and gratitude.

The LGBT community had a similar response to "The Puppy Episode." In her book, Betty recalls, "Many [gay men and women] said they watched in absolute wonder, not believing that this was finally happening on network TV." When Ellen's character publicly came out on national TV, many gay men and women felt happiness and relief. Betty also cites the reaction of actress and gay rights activist Amanda Bearse in *People* magazine: "The ice has been broken. We are in every job, we're every color. We're not out to take over the world. We just want to live in it."

CHAPTER 4

TWO ACCIDENTAL ACTIVISTS

"The most important thing in your life is to live your life with integrity and not to give into peer pressure, to try to be something that you're not. To live your life as an honest and compassionate person. To contribute in some way."—Ellen DeGeneres, Tulane University commencement speech

E llen DeGeneres wanted to have a right that heterosexuals already enjoyed: to be open and public about her sexual orientation. Her announcement contributed to political efforts that encouraged sensitivity and acceptance of the LGBT community.

ELLEN AND BETTY RESPOND

Ellen DeGeneres shared her sexual orientation with the public, but she did not anticipate the response that ensued. When the American Civil Liberties Union (ACLU) presented her with the Bill of Rights Award in

Betty DeGeneres speaks at the Gay and Lesbian Center's 33rd Anniversary Gala in Los Angeles.

1997, DeGeneres said, "I feel like I'm being honored for helping myself. I had no idea how many other lives would be affected by what [I'd] done... My decision to be honest parallels anyone in history who has stood up for his or her rights." DeGeneres's announcement became a platform for change in the United States. It encouraged gay people to publicly embrace being gay, rather than hide their sexual orientation.

DeGeneres's voice also prompted organizations that fight for equal rights for lesbians, gays, transgenders, and bisexuals to speak up. Lesbians and gay men are sexually attracted to others of the same gender. Bisexuals are attracted to both men and women. Transgenders include people who do not identify or express the gender of their birth. "I didn't choose to be anything other than a comedian," DeGeneres told *Time* magazine. "I just happen to be gay, and I didn't feel like keeping it a secret, so I announced it. It all turned into this whole big political thing." But in DeGeneres's coming out, "two accidental activists"— as gay rights activist Candace Gingrich called them, according to *Love, Ellen*—were born: Ellen and Betty.

The expression "being in the closet" means hiding from the outside world. Many LGBT people have been or still are "in the closet," which Betty once called "a stifling place to live." She reiterated these feelings in her book *Love, Ellen*: "Gay men and women have the same right to be out in the open, breathing the same air, as any of us." The Human Rights Campaign

(HRC) is the largest civil rights organization that promotes equality for the LGBT community. Betty embraced the HRC's approach of creating dialogues and open communication through the process of coming out.

In 1997, Betty became the HRC's first heterosexual spokesperson for National Coming Out Day. When Betty spoke out for this designated day, Ellen said, "To have a mom like this, not only to accept me and love me but to come out and be a spokesperson and travel—I'm so proud of her." Betty traveled around the country and visited cities including Los Angeles, Washington, D.C., Boston, Chicago, Portland, and Philadelphia as part of the Human Rights Campaign. Ellen also received one of the HRC's first National Civil Rights Awards.

According to the HRC site, "One out of every two Americans has someone close to them who is gay or lesbian." In coming out, gay people gain tremendous emotional and physical benefits already enjoyed by heterosexuals. And by listening to coming out stories, heterosexuals can increase their compassion and tolerance for people of all sexual orientations. In her book *Love, Ellen*, Betty also shared her feelings about being the HRC's National Coming Out Day spokesperson: "I had the chance to make a difference—to say 'enough,' enough of hatred and bigotry and ignorance and fear."

Betty honors this pledge by her involvement with the HRC and other LGBT organizations, such

BETTY'S ADVICE

In her book *Love, Ellen*, Betty gives advice to members of the gay community: gay men and women, parents of gay children, and children of gay parents. She talks about the things important to coming out, including having unconditional love, support, and acceptance; being honest, patient, and courageous; and using resources (such as organizations that support the LGBT community). She stresses that coming out is a personal decision that each person must do at his or her own time.

Betty offers a Turkish proverb to parents who have not accepted their children's gay orientation, "No matter how far you have gone on the wrong road, turn back." Being gay is not a choice, but how to live is a choice. Betty cites resources, such as PFLAG and high school clubs that help gay students to bond and address challenges. She also mentions the hotline and website TEEN LINE, where teens can receive help from other teens. Betty looks forward to a world where sexual orientation no longer matters. As she says, "What a blessing that will be!"

as Parents, Families and Friends of Lesbians and Gays (PFLAG), and Gay And Lesbian Alliance Against Defamation (GLAAD). From 1997 through the present, Betty has been speaking, traveling, and educating people. Throughout her work, she has met with gay rights allies, such as Representative Zoe Lofren from California, Joe Kennedy Jr., and Representative Richard Gephardt. Betty has become the voice of supportive parents of LGBT children everywhere. In a *Boston Spirit* article, writer David Zimmerman called Betty "America's mother." Betty agreed, "Yes, people always call me 'mama.'"

ELLEN'S TIMING

One year before DeGeneres announced she was gay, America passed the Defense of Marriage Act (DOMA), which legally defined marriage as the union between one man and one woman. When DeGeneres came out, she became part of a changing landscape. In a National Public Radio story, "How Ellen DeGeneres Helped Change the Conversation About Gays" by Lynn Neary, comedian and gay-rights activist Jessica Halem commented, "What's wonderful about her [Ellen], as a cultural figure, is that it worked so wonderfully along-side political activism. So there's political activism and cultural change going on at the same time."

DeGeneres received negative feedback from some members of the religious community. Baptist minister Jerry Falwell referred to DeGeneres as "Ellen Degenerate," implying that something was wrong with her because she was gay. DeGeneres responded with humor, stating, "Really, he called me that? Ellen Degenerate? I've been getting that since the fourth grade." And after DeGeneres became a judge on the popular show *American Idol*, Gary McCullough, director of Christian Newswire, predicted that the show would fail because Americans do not approve of "perverse behavior." When DeGeneres left the show in 2010—after only one season—McCullough remarked, "There is a limit to what Christian viewers will tolerate."

Despite McCullough's views, America's attitude toward different sexual orientations was changing. According to an ABC News/Washington Post poll, 58 percent of Americans supported gay marriage in 2013, up from 32 percent in 2004. DeGeneres and her mom were part of the catalyst for change both in heterosexuals' attitudes toward gay people and gay people's attitudes toward coming out. Ellen's and Betty's own comfort levels with Ellen's sexual orientation gave the LGBT community hope that they could publicly express themselves. It also provided LGBT organizations with other ways to openly support equal rights for all sexual orientations.

When DeGeneres first came out, she faced negative reactions from the entertainment world, advertisers for her show, and many American viewers. J.C. Penney was one of the advertisers to pull its funding from *Ellen* after "The Puppy Episode." But in 2012, she became the spokesperson for J.C. Penney. Michael Francis, former president of J.C. Penney Company, Inc., said, "Importantly, we share the same fundamental values

One of Degeneres's first jobs was working at J.C. Penney. Years later, she became the store's spokesperson.

as Ellen…The millions who watch her on television and follow her through social media relate to her and trust what she has to say."

As the J.C. Penney spokesperson, DeGeneres faced protests from One Million Moms, a division of the American Family Association (AFA). The AFA is a Christian organization that opposes gay marriage.

One Million Moms called on J.C. Penney to remove DeGeneres as its spokesperson because she is gay. The AFA further commented, "DeGeneres is not a true representation of the type of families that shop at their store. The majority of J.C. Penney shoppers will be offended and choose to no longer shop there."

J.C. Penney's response was in full support of DeGeneres. Its CEO, Ron Johnson, stated, "I think Ellen is someone we all trust. She's lovable, likable, honest and funny, but at her soul, we trust her." AdWeek further confirmed the changing tide: "Given the timeliness of the gay-marriage issue, it's not surprising to see brands take a stand, but when a classic American brand like J.C. Penney steps up, it's pretty clear where America is headed."

MORE ACTIVISM

As a child, Ellen loved animals. As an adult, she became a well-known animal rights activist, and her show has showcased other animal rights activists. For example, guests have spoken out against factory farming, which is a major cause of animal abuse. DeGeneres also hosted Wayne Pacelle, who is president of the Humane Society in the United States and the author of *The Bond*. The book discusses the special relationship between animals and humans, while also looking at ways to repair this relationship. On the episode "Ellen, For the Love of Animals," Pacelle

DISCRIMINATION AGAINST GAYS IN RUSSIA

In her 1997 ACLU speech, DeGeneres paraphrased a famous Martin Niemöller quote: "In Germany, the Nazis first came for the Communists and I didn't speak up because I wasn't a Communist; then they came for the Jews and I didn't speak up because I wasn't a Jew; then they came for the Catholics but I didn't speak up because I was a Protestant. Then they came for me and by that time there was no one left to speak for me." DeGeneres continued, "When will we learn? We could substitute any number of different groups and the principle remains the same, which is that it's a shame, that as far as we've come, we're still so intolerant and uncomfortable with diversity."

Russia is a place where intolerance and open discrimination against the LGBT community remains. In an article for *Slate*, "The Brutal, Bloody Horror of Gay Life in Putin's Russia," Mark Joseph Stern wrote, "Gay people in Russia are being beaten, raped, and murdered at record rates—and the government is doing little to stop it." This article cited data provided by Harvard University's *Health and Human Rights* journal and appeared on January 30, 2014, as Russia was preparing to host the Winter Olympics.

Russia has a history of discrimination against the LGBT community. In 2013, Russian president Vladimir Putin passed a law that prohibited "propaganda of nontraditional sexual practices" among minors. In practice, this law led to banning gay rights parades and excluding gays from television, newspapers, and magazines. And according to DoSomething.org, Russia tried to label being gay as a crime in 2002, 2003, and 2004. Gay people continue to be targeted for hate crimes, and when they have been victims of such crimes, many do not report them because they distrust the Russian police force.

In 2014, Russia hosted the XXII Olympic Winter Games. After many countries voiced concerns over Russia's discriminatory attitudes toward the LGBT community, Putin issued a statement that gay people would be safe if they "leave the children in peace." This comment was further evidence of Putin's offensive attitude toward gay people. Sarah Kate Ellis, president of GLADD, responded, "Mr. Putin can peddle fear and misinformation, but the global community is increasingly siding with equality for all people." President Obama sent a protest delegation to the Olympics that included gay U.S. athlete Billie Jean King.

Animal Rescue
adopt a shelter pet

USA 44

2010

The U.S. Postal Service provided this first-class stamp to promote adoption of animals in shelters.

called DeGeneres "an amazing animal advocate...the best friend of the Humane Society."

In 2009, People for the Ethical Treatment of Animals (PETA) named DeGeneres as its Woman of the Year. In 2011, Ellen received the Petco Foundation's HOPE Award, for her work to promote healthy bonds between people and animals. DeGeneres co-owns Halo, Purely for Pets, a natural food line for animals. Halo and DeGeneres partnered with the U.S. Postal Service to advance a stamp campaign aimed at increasing animal adoption. DeGeneres also worked with Halo to provide one million meals to animals in shelters. DeGeneres encourages others to get involved, too. She and her wife, Portia de Rossi, partnered with Alley Cat Allies to help feral cats, or domestic cats that are living in the wild. DeGeneres informs viewers of opportunities to support animal rights, such as a petition to end the yearly seal hunt in Canada.

Ellen DeGeneres visits
Australia's Taronga Zoo
with her wife, actress
Portia de Rossi.

In 2008, DeGeneres became a vegan, or a person who does not use or eat products made from animals. She features famous chefs on her show to share vegan recipes, such as Wolfgang Puck and Fabio Viviani. DeGeneres also makes vegan recipes available on her site, such as Kindness Week Vegan Cupcakes. This recipe does not use eggs, which come from chickens, or butter, which includes cow-produced milk. *Going Vegan with Ellen* is an online resource that helps people adopt and live a vegan-friendly lifestyle.

INNER STRENGTH

"I got to learn that I was strong enough to start over again."—Ellen DeGeneres, W Magazine

When Ellen DeGeneres announced that she was gay, the public's initial reaction hurt her career. But she did not give up. Her humor won back the hearts of television and movie producers and her fans. DeGeneres also appeared in print and television commercials. In 2003, the award-winning *The Ellen DeGeneres Show* first aired. In 2013, millions of people still tuned in to see DeGeneres.

LAUGHTER IS THE BEST MEDICINE

Despite the initial reaction to DeGeneres's coming out, she eventually returned to the entertainment world in a big way. In the *New York Times* article "Come Out. Come Down. Come Back. Being Ellen," Jesse Green cited the attitudes of Hollywood and the rest of

America, DeGeneres's ability to adapt, and her humor as factors that would determine the success of her comeback. In 2001, DeGeneres was put to the test when she returned as the host of the *53rd Annual*

Ellen DeGeneres brought much-needed laughter and smiles to many faces at the *53rd Annual Primetime Emmy Awards*, which aired shortly after the September 11 terrorist attacks.

Primetime Emmy Awards. The show was postponed twice following the September 11 terrorist attacks and security was high.

As host, DeGeneres had to deliver an entertaining

show while acknowledging both the attacks and the armed forces called upon to respond to them. On November 4 at the Shubert Theatre in Los Angeles, DeGeneres took the stage and said, "What would bug the Taliban more than seeing a gay woman in a suit surrounded by Jews?" By the end of the show, DeGeneres received a standing ovation.

In 2003, DeGeneres was one of nine comedians to cohost the *55th Annual Primetime Emmy Awards*, then in 2005, she hosted the *57th Annual Primetime Emmy Awards*, following Hurricane Katrina. "I guess I don't have to point out that this is the second time that I've hosted the Emmys after a national tragedy, and I just want to say

At the Emmy Awards, DeGeneres donned a swan outfit similar to the one worn by musician Björk at the Oscars.

that I'm honored because it's times like this that we really, really need laughter."

During the *53rd Annual Primetime Emmy Awards*, DeGeneres wore a swan dress. Her wardrobe poked fun at the outfit once donned by singer Björk. Given her preference for wearing pants, DeGeneres joked that it was good to wear a dress. According to the *New York Times* article by Sharon Waxman, when asked to host the Oscars, DeGeneres remarked, "Maybe I'll wear tux culottes. What do they call that? A skort?...I still have that swan dress sitting around."

ON THE AIR: MUSIC, DANCING, AND GENEROUS GIVEAWAYS

In 2003, DeGeneres launched a one-hour daytime television talk show called *The Ellen DeGeneres Show*. According to her show's site, "During its freshman season, 'The Ellen DeGeneres Show' ranked at the top of critics' lists, with *People*, *Entertainment Weekly*, the *New York Times*, *USA Today*, and *TV Guide* all citing the daytime talker as one of the best programs of 2003." DeGeneres incorporates humor into a broad array of subjects, while hosting numerous celebrities who often comprise Hollywood's A-list. Featured actors and actresses have included Brad Pitt, Halle Berry, Justin Timberlake, Reese Witherspoon, George Clooney, and Drew Barrymore.

On her show's site, DeGeneres cites musical appearances by the following:

- Beyoncé
- Lady Gaga
- Pink
- Mariah Carey
- The Black Eyed Peas
- Cher
- Madonna
- Paul McCartney

Seal is one of many musicians who have appeared on *The Ellen DeGeneres Show*.

- Prince
- Sir Elton John
- Mary J. Blige
- Keith Urban
- Taylor Swift
- Rascal Flatts

In 2010, DeGeneres also announced on her show that she was launching a record label, eleveneleven, with Telepictures. That year, eleveneleven signed Greyson Chance. This twelve-year-old sang "Waiting Outside the Lines" and received overnight fame. DeGeneres announced that the YouTube video of his performance, on the day he sang on the show, received 1.2 million views. By age fifteen, he was traveling around the world to promote his album, *Hold On 'Til the Night.* DeGeneres also signed seventeen-year-old Tom Andrews from the United Kingdom. He sang the James Brown song "It's a Man's Man's Man's World" on *The Ellen DeGeneres Show.* Other artists signed by eleveneleven include Savannah Robinson and duo Emily Luther and Charlie Puth. DeGeneres chose her record label's name because eleven was a number that kept popping up for her. It's not her ATM pin number, as she joked on her show.

DeGeneres also loves dancing. Zach Johnson reports, "Ellen DeGeneres was born to dance!" So are many of her guests! See www.ellentv.com to find videos of audience members dancing away (even during

First Lady Michelle Obama and Ellen DeGeneres dance to celebrate the second anniversary of the Let's Move initiative, which addresses childhood obesity.

commercial breaks). Guests offer solo performances and duets by men, women, and children, such as young Danny Keefe. DeGeneres and audience members have also danced with television's *So You Think You Can Dance* all-star DJ tWitch, who was the first guest DJ of season eleven of her show. Audience members can also sing on *The Ellen DeGeneres Show* and have performed songs, such as Katy Perry's "Roar" and Miley Cyrus's "Wrecking Ball." Everyone is at home on her set!

FINDING NEMO

In 2003, Ellen became the voice of *Finding Nemo*'s forgetful fish Dory. "I wrote it completely with [Ellen] in mind," Nemo director Andrew Stanton told the *Chicago Sun-Times*. The movie and DeGeneres's character were hits! *Finding Nemo* won Best Animated Feature at award shows, including:

- Academy Awards
- Academy of Science Fiction, Fantasy, & Horror
- Annie Awards
- New York Film Critics Online

Ellen DeGeneres won awards for her role as Dory, including Outstanding Voice Acting in an Animated Feature Production, in ceremonies sponsored by organizations including:

- Chicago Film Critics Association Awards
- Academy of Science Fiction, Fantasy, & Horror
- Annie Awards
- Kids' Choice Awards

The movie made $860 million. Ellen's character was such a huge hit that a sequel, *Finding Dory*, is scheduled for release in 2016. In the meantime, Dory would say, "Just keep swimming. Just keep swimming. Just keep swimming, swimming, swimming. What do we do? We swim, swim, swim."

DeGeneres's show offers a lot of giveaways. According to her show's site, gifts have included cash prizes ($10,000, $20,000, and $25,000), home makeovers, cars, and concert tickets. The "12 Days of Giveaways" show occur around Christmas. In 2013, the giveaways lasted thirteen days and ended December 23. DeGeneres gave away nearly $31,000 worth of gifts in

BE A PART OF HER SHOW!

In February 2014, DeGeneres offered several ways for viewers to get involved in her show:

Getting in Touch with Ellen: Provide advice to guests, showcase a talent (such as being a DJ, sharing a joke, or giving a picture for Dance Beat), or share experiences and knowledge. **Life Changing:** Reveal acts of kindness, surprise a loved one, provide an inspirational quote, or ask for help (such as with a home or paying for college).

Funny Videos: Post videos that highlight funny moments, life changing experiences, dance moves, or favorite viral videos.

Funny Pictures: Send in "What's Wrong With This Picture," funny police reports and newspaper clippings, bad tattoos, funny Facebook statuses, funny selfies, or bad school pictures.

Lifestyle: Submit favorite "Yelp reviews" on anything or favorite football fan photos.

Music: Send in a video and be considered for Ellen's record label, eleveneleven.

Talent, Ideas, and Games: Share your special, unusual skill or talent.

Animals: Send in pictures of animals.

Kids: Share funny kids' notes, first moments, videos, or art.

the first ten days. Prizes for the thirteen days included gift cards for Target, American Express, J.C. Penney, Whole Foods, Petco, Toys"R"Us, Visa, Zappos, and Hertz, as well as goods, such as vacation packages, a flat screen television, a camera, a laptop a computer, a tablet, a blender, cookware, and a Bulova watch with seventy-two diamonds.

In a 2014 HuffPost TV article, *Ellen DeGeneres Picks Her Top 10 Ellen Moments*, DeGeneres shared her show favorites. Her list included Britney Spears dancing "Gangnam Style," four-year-old Kai singing "Grenade," her *Finding Dory* announcement, *Friends* reunion with Jennifer Aniston, Kate McKinnon as host, and hidden pranks at Costco. In the *New York Post* article "10-Year-Old 'Ellen' Still a Hit" Michael Starr reported that ten years later, *The Ellen DeGeneres Show* averaged its best viewership since the show's launch—4.41 million viewers.

LOOK AT ME!

DeGeneres has also graced print ads and television commercials. In 2004, she agreed to participate in American Express's global advertising campaign that bore the tag "My life. My card." The campaign featured different famous people and individualized each ad to reflect the celebrity's life. DeGeneres's ads consisted of animals and humor. For example, her 2006 American Express commercial included pink flamingoes, Shelly the tortoise, a pig, an elephant, two hyenas, a dog, a bird, a goat, a giraffe, and Rikki the Raccoon. In an article for *The Inspiration Room*, Duncan Macleod notes that the ad ends with the phrase "My Life Goal: to work with animals," and is linked up with DeGeneres's final voice-over: "My life is far from ordinary. That's why my card is American Express."

American Express hired photographer Annie Leibovitz and famous director Martin Scorsese for the "My life. My card." ads. Later, Annie Leibovitz

Ellen DeGeneres and photographer Annie Leibovitz attend the American Express Global AD Campaign Launch Event. Leibovitz photographed Ellen a number of times.

also photographed DeGeneres for the first major American museum exhibit that portrayed art history from a gay perspective. The Hide/Seek: Difference and Desire in American Portraiture exhibit appeared at

the Smithsonian's National Portrait Gallery. But the exhibit's video, "Fire in My Belly," was withdrawn when the exhibit faced opposition from Republican House Speaker John Boehner and the Catholic League. In an article for the *Guardian*, Brian Logan cites art historian Jonathan Katz: "Will the decent majority of Americans stand against a fringe that sees censorship as a replacement for debate?" Hide/Seek sought to conquer what Katz called "the last acceptable prejudice in American political life."

DeGeneres has appeared in many publications, such as the *New York Times, USA Today, Time, TV Guide, Vanity Fair, Entertainment Weekly*, and *US Weekly*. She has also been on the covers of *W, People, Parade, Life, Allure, Redbook, Ladies' Home Journal, Los Angeles Magazine, Out, Shape,* and *Good Housekeeping.* In January 2009, DeGeneres announced that she wanted to grace the cover of *O, The Oprah Magazine*, which would be no small feat because only Oprah Winfrey herself appears on the cover of each issue of her magazine. Ellen launched her "O, Yes I Can!" campaign on her show, which included several humorous antics, including showing her viewing audience several mock *O* covers featuring herself with Oprah Winfrey. A couple months later, Oprah Winfrey asked Ellen to appear on the cover of *O* in a Skype request during the taping of the one thousandth episode of *Ellen*. History was made when the December 2009 issue of *O, The Oprah Magazine* came out featuring both women on the cover, and DeGeneres became one of only two people ever to share the magazine cover with Oprah Winfrey, sharing the honor with First Lady Michelle Obama.

CHAPTER 6

THAT WAS THEN, THIS IS NOW

"It's so important to say that out loud so people can also see for themselves how the things that broke you open actually allowed you to be set free."—Oprah Winfrey, The O Talks Collection

DeGeneres has hosted prestigious award shows, such as the Academy Awards, and she became the new face for CoverGirl cosmetics. But nothing touched DeGeneres's heart like marrying her partner, Portia de Rossi, when gay marriage became legal in California.

JUST KEEP SWIMMING...ALL THE WAY TO THE OSCARS

Like her character from *Finding Nemo*, DeGeneres keeps swimming. From the young woman who slept on a flea-infested mattress in 1980, DeGeneres had accumulated a net worth of $192 million by 2013. In 2007, she became the second woman ever to host

Finding Dory is the sequel to *Finding Nemo.* Ellen DeGeneres provided the voice for the character Dory.

the Academy Awards on her own. (Whoopi Goldberg was the first.) It was also the first time that an openly gay person hosted the award show. DeGeneres was an Academy Award host hit! She took her comedy routines to audience members: presenting a screenplay to best director Martin Scorsese, asking Steven Spielberg to take a picture of her with Clint Eastwood, and vacuuming the aisles.

In 2013, DeGeneres tweeted that she would once again host the Academy Awards. she joked, "I am so excited to be hosting the Oscars for the second time. You know what they say—the third time's the charm." In an official Oscars blog by Sanjit Das, the award show's producers, Craig Zadan and Neil Meron, said they were thrilled with DeGeneres's "gift of comedy, with her great warmth and humanity," and commented that she "is beloved everywhere." Dawn Hudson, CEO of the Academy of Motion Picture Arts and Sciences, also added, "[Ellen is] a big fan of the Oscars; we're huge fans of hers. It's a perfect match."

As the Oscars drew near, DeGeneres took to the streets in a trailer for the upcoming show. With 250

DeGeneres poses for a selfie at the 86th Annual Academy Awards with many actors.

people dressed in tuxedos, she danced and strutted to "The Walker" by Fitz and the Tantrums. DeGeneres also dressed in a Saint Laurent tux for promotional Oscar ads shared on Twitter. She added tweets such as "I'd like to thank The Academy. Seriously. Thank you," and "I be on my suit & tie..." In an Oscar blog by Valerie Ciliento, she read some of her favorite Twitter reactions to hosting the Oscars and offered some humorous responses. For example, when a viewer tweeted "OMG NO WAY I AM GOING TO DIE THIS IS JUST WAY TOO PERFECT I CAN'T EVEN OMG!!! CAN I COME?" DeGeneres remarked, "Try decaf." The 86th Oscars aired in March 2014 at the Hollywood's Dolby Theatre, and DeGeneres received rave reviews for her performance.

BEAUTIFUL COVERGIRL

In 2008, DeGeneres made another announcement on her show: she was the new face of CoverGirl cosmetics. The campaign with print and television ads began airing in January 2009. The campaign slogan was, "Easy, breezy, beautiful CoverGirl." DeGeneres is the face of Olay's Simply Ageless Foundation, a CoverGirl anti-aging product. Esi Eggleston Bracey, a vice president at Procter & Gamble, the parent company of CoverGirl, referred to DeGeneres as an "authentic beauty." The cosmetics company also signed other celebrities, including Queen Latifah, Pink, Katy Perry, and *Modern Family* star Sofía Vergara. In 2014, DeGeneres and Vergara teamed up for a commercial shoot in Germany (dubbed "Das Bombshell") for the CoverGirl Bombshell Volume by Lashblast Mascara.

Through CoverGirl, DeGeneres continues to help others. She assisted young cancer patient Talia Joy Castellano in becoming an honorary CoverGirl before she passed away at age thirteen in 2013. That year, eighteen-year-old Alexis Harris won the Ellen CoverGirl contest. She was chosen from almost twenty thousand applicants who submitted short descriptions and videos. Harris views her single mom as a positive inspiration. Harris also founded Students Making Impacts in Lives Everywhere (SMILE), which focuses on helping

Winner of the Ellen CoverGirl contest Alexis Harris was also a finalist in the TGI Fridays Red Hot Summer of Music Competition.

Ellen DeGeneres celebrates CoverGirl's fiftieth anniversary with talented celebrities Taylor Swift, Drew Barrymore, Dania Ramirez, and Queen Latifah.

others with efforts such as food and clothing drives. She cited Ellen as motivating her to help others, and Ellen believed that Harris's selfless spirit was

exactly what the contest was looking for in a CoverGirl.

According to the CoverGirl site, DeGeneres's preferred products in 2014 included CoverGirl + Olay Tone Rehab 2-in-1 foundation, pressed powder, and concealer balm. Animal testing is an issue in the cosmetics industry, and DeGeneres is a strong animal activist. According to People for Ethical Treatment of Animals (PETA), CoverGirl products are not tested on animals—although these products are sold in countries that allow animal testing for cosmetics (including China).

SO YOU THINK YOU CAN SING?

In 2009, the network FOX announced that DeGeneres would become a fourth judge on the popular TV talent show *American Idol.* Following Paula Abdul's departure, DeGeneres joined Simon Cowell, Randy Jackson, and Kara DioGuardi for the show's ninth season.

Before joining the panel, DeGeneres had been a guest judge on *So You Think You Can Dance* with the top eight finalists and had cohosted the star-studded show *Idol Gives Back*, which helped raise money for impoverished young people in America and Africa through the Charity Projects Entertainment Fund.

DeGeneres brought her passion for music to the *American Idol* judges' panel. Executive producers felt that she also brought warmth and compassion to the show. In 2010, DeGeneres told both FOX and the show's producers of her decision to leave. In an *US Weekly* article she said, "I also realized this season that while I love discovering, support-ing and nurturing young talent, it was hard for me to judge and sometimes hurt their feelings. I loved the experience working on *Idol* and I am very grate-ful for the year I had..."

In 2014, DeGeneres was still keeping her audi-ence in the *American Idol* loop. For example, she hosted *American Idol*'s Season 13 judges Keith Urban, Jennifer Lopez, and Harry Connick Jr. on her own show. DeGeneres also invited viewers to comment on the judges' call concerning twenty-two-year-old Jessica Bassett. DeGeneres disagreed with the "no" votes from Harry Connick Jr. and Keith Urban for Bassett. (Jennifer Lopez gave her a "yes.") she responded by extending an invitation for Bassett to sing on *The Ellen DeGeneres Show*.

ANOTHER MAGAZINE COVER: A WEDDING!

DeGeneres and actress Portia de Rossi began dating at the end of 2004. In coming out publicly as

HEADS UP

In October 2012, producers of *The Ellen DeGeneres Show* hired an iPhone, iPad, and iPod touch app development studio called Impending. The producers wanted to turn a game that DeGeneres and her guests played into an app called *Heads Up.* How is the game played on the show? DeGeneres holds a card with a word or phrase up to her forehead. The guest then supplies clues aimed at Ellen successfully guessing the word. Now that the app is out, DeGeneres sometimes plays on her show holding an iPad in front of her, as she did when she challenged Harry Connick Jr. to a game.

The app works the same way. A person holds a mobile phone up to his or her forehead. The other player(s) sees the word and gives clues. The person holding the device has one minute to guess as many words as possible. He or she tips the tablet or phone to get a new card. There are eighteen "decks," or categories, from which to choose, including celebrities, sports legends, accents and impressions, blockbuster movies, songs, and animals. The app can film the games' sessions, which can then be shared on social media sites such as Facebook or sent directly to DeGeneres (who may air them on her show).

DeGeneres has played *Heads Up* on the air with celebrities, including Owen Wilson, Adam Levine, Lauren Graham, Robin Williams, and Alison Sweeney. When playing with Alison Sweeney, one of the phrases was "Portia de Rossi" and DeGeneres's clue was "She's married to me." After DeGeneres announced *Heads Up* on her Twitter account in 2013, it soared to the number one spot on Apple's best-selling apps list. The iTunes page for *Heads Up* reveals that *Cosmopolitan* magazine called the app "the best dollar you've spent" and the *New York Times* believes it's a "sensation."

DeGeneres's love interest, de Rossi also came out as a gay woman. As reported by CNN's Breeanna Hare, "'Ellen and I had been together for a month, and I was very, very nervous going to that [Golden Globes] because I knew that I was going to meet up with her after the show and that there was press,' de Rossi continued. 'That was the first time that we actually stepped out together as a couple, but for me, it was the first time that I'd stepped out as a gay woman, really.'"

On a heartwarming *Oprah Winfrey* show, DeGeneres described de Rossi as the "smartest, kindest, most wonderful woman that you'll ever, ever know." De Rossi shared knowing that DeGeneres was the one when "she laid eyes on her," but it took her three years to speak up because she had not yet come out. De Rossi said she was worried about the professional repercussions of coming out and dating a well-known lesbian. But the connection between the women was there. DeGeneres and de Rossi were set to have a commitment ceremony during a joint birthday party. But when gay marriage became legal in California, it turned into a wedding!

Their wedding was August 17, 2008. DeGeneres was fifty, and her bride was thirty-five. The two exchanged handwritten vows in a small ceremony with only nineteen guests, including Betty

DeGeneres. They dined on an all-vegan meal and red velvet cake. Their wedding picture graced the cover of *People* magazine, and the public reaction was very different than years before, when DeGeneres came out on the cover of *Time* magazine. This time, DeGeneres's viewers, her show's sponsors, and most of America celebrated with her.

Ellen DeGeneres and Portia de Rossi wed in a small ceremony in their backyard.

TIMELINE

1958 Ellen DeGeneres is born on January 26 in Metaire, Louisiana, a suburb of New Orleans.

1978 DeGeneres first discusses her sexual orientation with her mother.

1982 DeGeneres wins Showtime's Funniest Person in America contest.

1986 DeGeneres becomes the first female stand-up comic to be invited to sit down on *The Tonight Show Starring Johnny Carson*.

1989 DeGeneres lands a regular TV role on the Fox sitcom *Duet*, and its spin-off, *Open House*.

1991 DeGeneres wins Best Female Stand-Up at the American Comedy Awards.

1994 DeGeneres stars in the television series *These Friends of Mine*. The show is renamed *Ellen* in its second season.

1995 DeGeneres publishes her first book, *My Point...And I Do Have One*, which debuts at #1 on the *New York Times* best-sellers list.

1997 Both in her private life and on the *Ellen* TV show, DeGeneres announces that she is gay. She also wins her first Emmy and receives the American Civil Liberties Union's Bill of Rights Award.

2001 DeGeneres hosts the *53rd Annual Primetime Emmy Awards*, following the September 11 terrorist attacks.

2003 DeGeneres launches *The Ellen DeGeneres Show*. The show earns thirty-five Daytime Emmy Awards in its first eight seasons.
DeGeneres becomes the voice of Dory in the Oscar's Best Animated Feature *Finding Nemo*.

2004 DeGeneres agrees to participate in American Express's global ad campaign.

2005 DeGeneres hosts the *57th Annual Primetime Emmy Awards*, following Hurricane Katrina.

2007 DeGeneres becomes the second woman to host the Academy Awards.

2008 DeGeneres marries actress Portia de Rossi when gay marriage becomes legal in California; becomes the new face of CoverGirl cosmetics; and wins Television Week's Syndication Personality of the Year.

2009 DeGeneres receives Woman of the Year from People for Ethical Treatment of Animals (PETA).

2010 DeGeneres becomes the fourth judge on *American Idol*. Degeneres begins her own record label, eleveneleven, with Telepictures.

2012 DeGeneres became the spokesperson for J.C. Penney. She releases the app *Heads Up*.

2013 DeGeneres is named one of *Forbes* 100 Most Powerful Women.

2014 DeGeneres hosts the Academy Awards. Her "selfie" from the show breaks a Twitter record.

GLOSSARY

ACTIVIST A person who uses campaigning to bring about social change.

ADVOCATE A person who supports a specific cause.

BISEXUAL Being attracted to both men and women.

COMEDY Professional entertainment intended to make an audience laugh.

COMEDY CLUB A place for comedians to perform live in front of an audience.

COMING OUT When lesbians, gays, bisexuals, and transgender people publicly announce their sexual orientation or gender identity.

DISCRIMINATION Treatment of a person based on race, religion, sexual orientation or other category, rather than individual merit.

DOCUMENTARY A movie, radio program, or television program based on factual information.

EMCEE A person who hosts an entertainment event.

GAY Sexually attracted to people of the the same gender.

GENDER Being either female or male.

HETEROSEXUAL Sexually attracted to people of the opposite gender.

IN THE CLOSET Expression used to describe a gay person who has not publicly disclosed his or her sexual orientation.

INTOLERANCE Not willing to entertain views different from one's own.

LESBIAN A woman who is attracted to other women.

MONOLOGUE A routine or speech performed by one person.

OPTIMIST A person who is hopeful about the future.

ORIENTATION The direction of someone's interest, attraction, or ability, particularly political or sexual.

PREJUDICE Unfair treatment based on unfounded opinions.

PROMO An advertising clip, such as a short video.

SENSITIVITY Awareness of others' reactions and feelings.

SEXUAL ORIENTATION Tendency of a person to be heterosexual, homosexual, or bisexual.

SKIT A humorous sketch or short dramatic story.

STAND-UP COMEDY Comedy performed alone in front of a live audience.

TRANSGENDER People who do not identify or express the gender of their birth.

UNCONDITIONAL Not limited or bound in any way.

American Civil Liberties Union (ACLU)
125 Broad Street, 18th Floor
New York, NY 10004
(212) 549-2500
Website: http://www.aclu.org
The ACLU works in courts, legislatures, and com-
   munities to defend the rights and liberties of
   all individuals. It seeks to extend rights to
   those traditionally denied, like the lesbian,
   gay, bisexual, and transgender (LGBT)
   community.

Central Toronto Youth Services
65 Wellesley Street East
Suite 300
Toronto, ON M4Y 1G7
Canada
(416) 924-2100
Website: http://www.ctys.org
The community-based Central Toronto Youth Services
   (CTYS) is dedicated to helping troubled youth,
   including those coping with "issues of sexual
   orientation and gender identity."

Community One Foundation
P.O. Box 760, Station F
Toronto, ON M4Y 2N6
Canada
(416) 920-5422
Website: http://communityone.ca
This foundation supports individuals and groups that
   promote the development of the LGBT community
   in the greater Toronto area.

Gay-Straight Alliance (GSA) Network
1550 Bryant Street, Suite 600
San Francisco, CA 94103
(415) 552-4229
Website: http://www.gsanetwork.org
The Gay-Straight Alliance Network endeavors to put
   school-based Gay-Straight Alliances (GSAs) in
   touch with one another as well as "community
   resources through peer support, leadership development, and training."

Human Rights Campaign (HRC)
1640 Rhode Island Avenue NW
Washington, DC 20036-3278
(800) 777-4723
Website: http://www.hrc.org
The HRC is the largest civil rights organization dedicated to promoting equality for the LGBT
   community.

Humane Society of the United States
2100 L Street NW
Washington, DC 20037
(866) 720-2676
Website: http://www.humanesociety.org
The Humane Society is the largest animal protection
   organization in the United States.

Lesbian Gay Bi Trans Youth Line
P.O. Box 62, Station F
Toronto, ON M4Y 2L4
Canada
(800) 268-9688

Website: http://www.youthline.ca
The youth-run Lesbian Gay Bi Trans Youth Line is a
    hotline for the concerns of all youth, ready to
    answer any and all questions and address any
    concerns.

Parents, Families and Friends of Lesbians and
    Gays (PFLAG)
PFLAG National Office
1828 L Street NW, Suite 660
Washington, DC 20036
(202) 467-8180
Website: http://www.pflag.org
As the nation's largest family and ally organization,
    PFLAG supports the health and well-being of
    members of the LGBT community.

People for the Ethical Treatment of Animals (PETA)
501 Front Street
Norfolk, VA 23510
(757) 622-7382
Website: http://www.peta.org
PETA is the largest animal rights organization around
    the globe.

Point Foundation
5757 Wilshire Boulevard, Suite 370
Los Angeles, CA 90036
and
1357 Broadway, Suite 401
New York, NY 10018
(866) 337-6468
Website: http://www.pointfoundation.org

As the national LGBTQ scholarship foundation, the Point Foundation helps promising LGBTQ students to achieve their academic and leadership potential.

Supporting Our Youth (SOY)
333 Sherbourne Street, 2nd Floor
Toronto, ON M5A 2S5
Canada
(416) 324-5077
Website: http://www.soytoronto.org
SOY works to improve the lives of youth in the LGBT community.

WEBSITES

Because of the changing nature of Internet links, Rosen Publishing has developed an online list of websites related to the subject of this book. This site is updated regularly. Please use this link to access the list:

http://www.rosenlinks.com/GLBT/DeGen

Bacon, Quentin, Ellen DeGeneres, Roberto Martin, and Portia de Rossi. *Vegan Cooking for Carnivores: Over 125 Recipes So Tasty You Won't Miss the Meat.* New York, NY: Grand Central Life & Style, 2013.

Belge, Kathy, and Marke Bieschke. *Queer: The Ultimate LGBT Guide for Teens.* San Francisco, CA: Zest Books, 2011.

Bialik, Mayim, and Jay Gordon. *Mayim's Vegan Table: More than 100 Great-Tasting and Healthy Recipes from My Family to Yours.* Boston, MA: Da Capo Press, 2014.

Cooke, C. W. *Female Force: Women in the Media: A Graphic Biography Novel.* Beverly Hills, CA: Bluewater Production, 2010.

DeGeneres, Betty. *So Far So... Terrific: A Memoir and More.* Seattle, WA: CreateSpace Independent Publishing Platform, 2012.

DeGeneres, Ellen. *My Point...And I Do Have One.* New York, NY: Bantam Books, 2007.

DeGeneres, Ellen. *Seriously...I'm Kidding.* New York, NY: Grand Central Publishing, 2011.

Elise, Kerry. *Ellen Degeneres: The Best of Ellen Degeneres: Secrets on Life, Love, and Laughter.* Seattle, WA: Amazon Digital Services, Inc., 2014.

Gragg, Adam, Patrick McCray, Sandra Ruckdeschel, and Marc Shapiro. *Female Force: Women of Comedy.* Beverly Hills, CA: Bluewater Production, 2012.

Huegel, Kelly. *GLBTQ: The Survival Guide for Gay, Lesbian, Bisexual, Transgender, and Questioning Teens.* Minneapolis, MN: Free Spirit Publishing, Inc., 2011.

Melendez, Macie. *Ellen DeGeneres: A Biography.* San Francisco, CA: Hyperink, 2012. Kindle ed.

Moskowitz, Isa Chandra. *Isa Does It: Amazingly Easy, Wildly Delicious Vegan Recipes for Every Day of the Week.* New York, NY: Little, Brown and Company, 2012.

Orr, Tamra B. *Home and Family Relationships* (Teens: Being Gay, Lesbian, Bisexual, or Transgender). New York, NY: Rosen Publishing, 2010.

Paprocki, Sherry Beck. *Ellen Degeneres: Entertainer* (Women of Achievement). New York, NY: Chelsea House Publishers, 2009.

Risley, April. *Electric, Eccentric & Esoteric Ellen: The Biography of Ellen Degeneres.* Seattle, WA: Amazon Digital Services, Inc., 2012.

Sharp, Katie. *Ellen DeGeneres* (People in the News). San Diego, CA: Lucent Books, 2010.

Sickels, Robert C. *100 Entertainers Who Changed America: An Encyclopedia of Pop Culture Luminaries.* Santa Barbara, CA: Greenwood, 2013.

Simpton, Hy. *Ellen DeGeneres Spotlight: Dancing, Judging and Laughing.* Seattle, WA: Amazon Digital Services, Inc., 2013.

Smith, T. *Ellen DeGeneres... From Beginning to Now.* Seattle, WA: Amazon Digital Services, Inc., 2012.

Stewart, Jessica. *Ellen DeGeneres: 110 Facts You Need to Know!* Seattle, WA: Amazon Digital Services, Inc., 2013.

Worth, Richard. *Life at School and in the Community* (Teens: Being Gay, Lesbian, Bisexual, or Transgender). New York, NY: Rosen Publishing, 2010.

Ciliento, Valerie. "Ellen Reads Twitter Reactions to Her Hosting the 2014 Oscars." The Oscars, January 14, 2014. Retrieved February 2014 (http://oscar.go .com/blogs/oscar-blogs-general/ellen-degeneres -hosting-2014-oscars-twitter-reactions).

CoverGirl. "Ellen DeGeneres." Retrieved February 2014 (http://www.covergirl.com/covergirl-models/ellen -degeneres-covergirl).

Das, Sanjit. "Ellen DeGeneres Returns to Host the Oscars." The Oscars, August 2, 2013. Retrieved February 2013 (http://oscar.go.com/blogs/oscar -news/ellen-degeneres-returns-to-host-the-oscars).

Davis, Monique. "Alexis Harris Wins Ellen DeGeneres 2013 CoverGirl Contest." *Atlanta Black Star*, March 8, 2013. Retrieved February 2014 (http:// atlantablackstar.com/2013/03/08/alexis-harris-wins -ellen-degeneres-2013-covergirl-contest).

DeGeneres, Betty. *Love, Ellen: A Mother/Daughter Journey.* New York, NY: William Morrow and Company, 1999.

DeGeneres, Ellen. "Coming Out." October 8, 2013. Retrieved January 2014 (http://ellen012.blogspot .com/2013/10/coming-out.html).

DeGeneres, Ellen. *My Point...And I Do Have One.* New York, NY: Bantam, 2007.

DeGeneres, Ellen. *The Funny Thing Is...* New York, NY: Simon & Schuster, 2003.

DeGeneres, Ellen. "Tragedy to Triumph." October 8, 2013. Retrieved January 2014 (http://ellen012 .blogspot.com/2013/10/tragedy-to-triumph.html).

EllenTV.com. "The Ellen DeGeneres Show." Retrieved February 2014 (http://www.ellentv.com).

Foley, Bridget. "Ellen DeGeneres." *W*, March 2007. Retrieved January 2014 (http://www

.wmagazine.com/people/celebrities/2007/03/
ellen_degeneres).

Ford, Rebecca. "Oscars: Ellen DeGeneres' Hosting
History." *Hollywood Reporter*, August 2, 2013.
Retrieved January 2014 (http://www
.hollywoodreporter.com/news/oscars-ellen-degeneres
-hosting-history-598767).

Goodreads. "Ellen DeGeneres quotes." Retrieved
February 2014 (http://www.goodreads.com/author/
quotes/40648.Ellen_DeGeneres).

Gradspeeches. "Ellen DeGeneres Graduation Speech –
Video & Transcript." May 16, 2009. Retrieved
January 2014 (http://gradspeeches.com/2009/
tulane-university/ellen-degeneres).

Green, Jesse. "Come Out. Come Down. Come Back.
Being Ellen." *New York Times*, August 19, 2001.
Retrieved January 2014 (http://www.nytimes.com/
2001/08/19/magazine/come-out-come-down-come
-back-being-ellen.html).

Hare, Breeanna. "Portia de Rossi: The First Time I Truly
Came Out." CNN, November 8, 2013. Retrieved
February 2014 (http://www.cnn.com/2013/11/08/
showbiz/celebrity-news-gossip/portia-de-rossi-gay).

Herek, Gregory M. "Stigma, Prejudice, and Violence
Against Lesbians and Gay Men." Retrieved February
2014 (http://psychology.ucdavis.edu/faculty_sites/
rainbow/html/spssi_91.pdf).

Hollander, Barbara Gottfried. *Marriage Rights and Gay
Rights: Interpreting the Constitution* (Understanding
the United States Constitution). New York, NY:
Rosen Publishing, 2014.

Huffington Post. "Ellen DeGeneres' JC Penney
Partnership Slammed by Anti-Gay Group One
Million Moms." February 1, 2012. Retrieved

January 2014 (http://www.huffingtonpost.com/
2012/02/01/ellen-degeneres-jc-penney_n_
1247657.html).

Huffington Post. "Ellen DeGeneres Picks Her Top 10
Ellen Moments." August 20, 2013. Retrieved
January 2014 (http://www.huffingtonpost
.com/hulucom/ellen-degeneres-picks-her_b_
3781823.html).

Huffington Post. "Oprah Winfrey: After Ellen DeGeneres'
Coming Out Episode, I Was Called the N Word."
August 22, 2012. Retrieved February 2014 (http://
www.huffingtonpost.com/2012/08/22/oprah-ellen
-degerenes-coming-out-n-word_n_1822961.html).

Human Rights Campaign. "National Coming Out Day."
Retrieved January 2014 (http://www.hrc.org/
resources/entry/national-coming-out-day).

Iannucci, Lisa. *Ellen DeGeneres: A Biography.* Westport,
CT: Greenwood Press, 2009.

IMDb. "Anne Heche." Retrieved February 2014 (http://
www.imdb.com/name/nm0000162).

IMDb. "Ellen DeGeneres." Retrieved January 2014
(http://www.imdb.com/name/nm0001122).

IMDb. "Ellen (TV Series 1994–1998)." Retrieved January 2014 (http://www.imdb.com/title/tt0108761).

IMDb. "Finding Nemo Awards." Retrieved February
2014 (http://www.imdb.com/title/tt0266543/awards).

IMDb. "Vance DeGeneres." Retrieved February 2014
(http://www.imdb.com/name/nm0214699/?ref_=
nv_sr_1).

Infoplease. "The American Gay Rights Movement: A
Timeline." Retrieved January 2014 (http://www
.infoplease.com/ipa/A0761909.html).

It Gets Better Project. "President Obama: It Gets
Better." Retrieved February 2014 (http://www
.itgetsbetter.org/video/entry/geyafbsdpvk).

JCPenney. "Company News." Retrieved February 2014 (http://ir.jcpenney.com/phoenix.zhtml ?c=70528&p=irol-newsArticle&ID=1652606 &highlight=).

Jensen, Kurt. "Ellen's Mom Tells of Rough 'Journey.'" *USA Today*, December 2, 1999. Retrieved February 2014 (http://usatoday30.usatoday.com/life/enter/ books/b1078.htm).

Johnson, Zach. "Ellen DeGeneres Dances in the Street – Watch the Host's Oscars Trailer!" Eonline, December 20, 2013. Retrieved February 2014 (http://www.eonline.com/news/492805/ellen -degeneres-dances-in-the-street-watch-the-host-s -oscars-trailer).

Kerr, Michael. "Depression and Sexual Orientation." Healthline, March 29, 2012. Retrieved January 2014 (http://www.healthline.com/health/ depression/gay).

Lally, Kathy. "Putin: Gay People Will Be Safe at Olympics If They 'Leave Kids Alone.'" *Washington Post*, January 17, 2014. Retrieved February 2014 (http://www.washingtonpost.com/world/putin-gays -will-be-safe-at-olympics-if-they-leave-kids-alone/ 2014/01/17/e6f8c47e-7f7d-11e3-95c6 -0a7aa80874bc_story.html).

Lang, Derrick J. "Ellen DeGeneres Joining 'American Idol' As 4th Judge." *Huffington Post*, September 10, 2009. Retrieved February 2014 (http://www .huffingtonpost.com/2009/09/09/ellen-degeneres -joining-a_n_281466.html).

Langer, Gary. "Poll Tracks Dramatic Rise In Support for Gay Marriage." *ABC News/Washington Post*, March 18, 2013. Retrieved January 2014 (http://abcnews .go.com/blogs/politics/2013/03/poll-tracks-dramatic -rise-in-support-for-gay-marriage).

Logan, Brian. "Hide/Seek: Too Shocking for America." *Guardian*, December 5, 2010. Retrieved February 2014 (http://www.theguardian.com/artanddesign/ 2010/dec/05/hide-seek-gay-art-smithsonian).

Macleod, Duncan. "American Express and Ellen DeGeneres Win with Animals." Inspiration Room, May 12, 2007. Retrieved February 2014 (http:// theinspirationroom.com/daily/2007/american -express-ellen-degeneres).

Mantyla, Kyle. "Ellen DeGeneres' Gayness Destroyed American Idol!" Right Wing Watch, July 30, 2010. Retrieved January 2014 (http://www.rightwingwatch .org/content/ellen-degeneres-gayness-destroyed -american-idol).

Melendez, Macie. *Biography of Ellen DeGeneres.* San Francisco, CA: Hyperink, 2012.

Neary, Lynn. "How Ellen DeGeneres Helped Change the Conversation About Gays." NPR, March 25, 2013. Retrieved February 2014 (http://www.npr .org/2013/03/25/175265720/how-ellen -degeneres-helped-change-the-conversation -about-gays).

The O Talks Collection. "Oprah Talks to Ellen DeGeneres." Retrieved February 2014 (http://www .oprah.com/omagazine/Oprah-Interviews-Ellen -DeGeneres-Ellens-O-Magazine-Cover/2).

People. "Ellen DeGeneres." Retrieved January 2014 (http://www.people.com/people/ellen_degeneres/ biography).

Queerty. "Oprah Listens Intently as Ellen + Portia Share Their Lesbian Love Story." November 10, 2009. Retrieved February 2014 (http://www.queerty.com/ oprah-listens-intently-as-ellen-portia-share-their -lesbian-love-story-20091110).

The Richest. "Ellen DeGeneres Net Worth." Retrieved February 2014 (http://www.therichest.com/ celebnetworth/celeb/tv-personality/ellen-degeneres -net-worth).

Soriano, César G. "Ellen Opens Up About Her Past." *USA Today*, May 18, 2005. Retrieved January 2014 (http://usatoday30.usatoday.com/life/people/2005 -05-18-degeneres_x.htm).

Southeast Missourian. "Ellen Suffered Depression." December 1, 1998. Retrieved February 2014 (http://news.google.com/newspapers?nid=1893&dat =19981201&id=35EkAAAAIBAJ&sjid=w9wFAAAAI BAJ&pg=2175,4995967).

Stern, Mark Joseph. "The Brutal, Bloody Horror of Gay Life in Putin's Russia." *Slate*, January 30, 2014. Retrieved February 2014 (http://www.slate.com/ blogs/outward/2014/01/30/gay_russia_under_putin _brutal_bloody_and_horrifying.html).

Tracy, Kathleen. *Ellen: The Real Story of Ellen DeGeneres.* New York, NY: Pinnacle Books, 2005.

Waxman, Sharon. "Ellen DeGeneres Is Chosen as Host of Next Year's Oscars." *New York Times*, September 9, 2006. Retrieved January 2014 (http://www .nytimes.com/2006/09/09/movies/09elle.html).

Weinstein, Joshua. "One Million Moms to JC Penney: Ellen's Gay — Fire Her." The Wrap, February 1, 2012. Retrieved January 2014 (http://www.thewrap .com/tv/article/american-family-association-ellens -gay-fire-her-35019).

Zimmerman, David. "'America's Mom' Betty DeGeneres Discusses Ellen, Parenting, and Lady Gaga." Boston. com, April 30, 2012. Retrieved January 2014 (http://www.boston.com/lifestyle/blogs/bostonspirit/ 2012/04/americas_mom_betty_degeneres_d.html).

INDEX